What ancient city was destroyed but never attacked?

Where can you find seas that are not seas?

How can you draw a straight line that is curved?

What has no mouth but eats?

Join the enthusiastic and creative Professor Egghead as he entertains you with his selection of brainteasing riddles on history, geography, mathematics, and science. Delightful illustrations by an award-winning cartoonist add to the fun of the Professor's tantalizing puzzlers.

PROFESSOR EGGHEAD'S BEST RIDDLES
was originally published by
Simon and Schuster.

Critics' Corner:

About the Author and Illustrator:

ROSE WYLER, who is well known for her many science books for young readers, has taught elementary science in New York public schools and science education at Columbia Teachers College; she has also done field work in astronomy, biology, and geology. She is co-author with her husband, Gerald Ames, of *The Giant Golden Book of Astronomy* and *The Giant Golden Book of Biology,* as well as the author of many books of science and math puzzles. Ms. Wyler and her husband have three children and three grandchildren. They live in New York City during the winter and spend their summers in Maine.

JERRY ROBINSON, creator of the nationally syndicated cartoons *Still Life* and *Flubs & Fluffs,* has written a number of books and illustrated over 30 of them. Mr. Robinson is a past president of the National Cartoonists Society, has won numerous awards for his work, including the coveted Ruben Award in three separate categories, and is the author of the definitive work *The Comics: An Illustrated History of 75 Years of Comic Strip Art.* Mr. Robinson is married, has a daughter and a son, and lives in New York City.

PROFESSOR EGGHEAD'S BEST RIDDLES

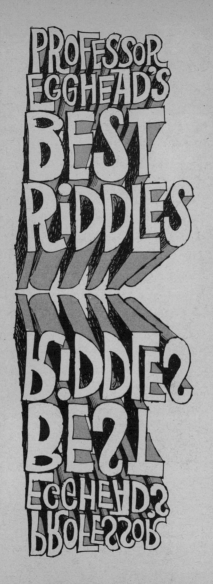

PROFESSOR EGGHEAD'S BEST RIDDLES

AN ARCHWAY PAPERBACK
POCKET BOOKS · NEW YORK

A reflection
in water

A reflection
in water

PROFESSOR EGGHEAD'S BEST RIDDLES

Simon and Schuster edition published 1973

Archway Paperback edition published February, 1975

Published by **POCKET BOOKS**, a division of Simon & Schuster, Inc., 630 Fifth Avenue, New York, N.Y. Archway Paperback editions are distributed in the U.S. by Simon & Schuster, Inc., 630 Fifth Avenue, New York, N.Y. 10020, and in Canada by Simon & Schuster of Canada, Ltd., Markham, Ontario, Canada.

Standard Book Number: 671-29709-0.
Library of Congress Catalog Card Number: 77-179991.
Printed in the U.S.A.

CONTENTS

Dear Reader:

As you may know, I am the world's leading expert in Riddleography. I have done research in 27½ countries, trying to find out which is the more important part of a riddle—the question or the answer.

While at work on this problem, I became interested in a type of riddle known as the true riddle. In this type, the question is usually foolish but the answer is sensible. Such riddles are therefore of great educational value, and

I began using them in my teaching. Soon I was making up true riddles of my own.

These are my favorites. One of my pupils, Rose Wyler, polished them up a bit and grouped them according to the subjects they cover. She also carefully checked the accuracy of the answers, although there was no need of that. Anyway, my thanks to her for her trouble. Thanks also to another pupil, Jerry Robinson, for his illustrations. Although he was always drawing while I was lecturing, he got the point of the riddles. But I do regret that he did not make me as handsome as I really am.

Sincerely yours,

Professor Egghead

Professor Egghead, A.B.C., DEF., C.O.D.

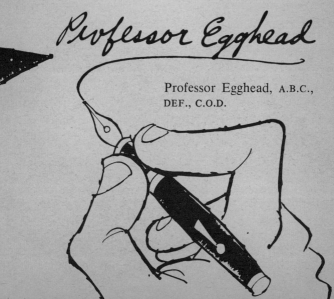

HISTORY

What great explorer did not know where he was going, or where he was when he got there, or where he had been when he got back?

Columbus.

He thought he was on his way to Asia when he really was headed for America.

He thought he was in Asia when he landed on the island of San Salvador. He called the people there Indians, for he believed he had reached India.

And Columbus died without knowing where he really had been.

Two famous members of the Roosevelt family stood in front of the White House. Both called Theodore Roosevelt "uncle" but one was the father of the other one's son. What relation were they to each other?

Husband and wife.

They were Franklin and Eleanor Roosevelt, who were distant cousins. Theodore Roosevelt was Eleanor's father's brother and therefore her uncle. Franklin called him "uncle" too, after marrying Eleanor.

As you may know, Franklin and Eleanor Roosevelt had several children—four sons and one daughter.

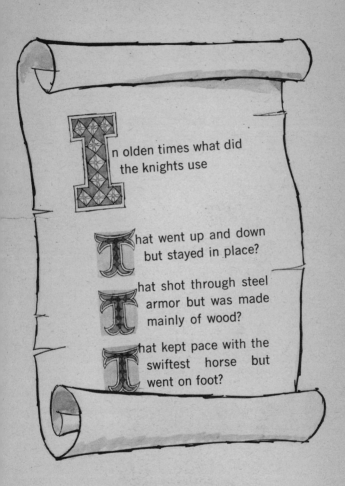

In olden times what did the knights use

That went up and down but stayed in place?

That shot through steel armor but was made mainly of wood?

That kept pace with the swiftest horse but went on foot?

A drawbridge.

Each castle was surrounded by a moat. The only way to get over it was to cross a drawbridge. If the bridge was raised, no one could enter the castle.

A crossbow.
This powerful bow was drawn back by means of a winder. It shot steel-tipped arrows that could go through armor.

Spurs.
A knight wore spurs on his boots to prod his horse. Only knights and nobles were allowed spurs.

What is in the Great Wall of China that the Chinese never put there?

Cracks.

How
did it
happen . . .

—that a famous group of explorers crossed the North Pole but never saw the North Star?

—that the U.S. Army used an aircraft carrier long before airplanes were invented?

—that a great expedition covered only 10 miles?

The explorers traveled under the ice of the Arctic Ocean.
They were aboard the U.S.S. *Nautilus* in 1958 on the first submarine expedition to cross the North Pole.

The aircraft was a balloon and the carrier, a tugboat named Fanny.

In 1861 a balloon rose from her deck, carrying a Union soldier on an observation flight over Virginia. This was the first time an aircraft was used in warfare.

The expedition was the first trip into the stratosphere.

Auguste Piccard made the ascent in 1931 in a sealed gondola, dangling from a big balloon. Jet planes now fly in the region that he explored.

Here is a riddle from Revolutionary days:

Why did George Washington say he could make a dollar go farther than anyone else?

Because he once threw a silver dollar across the Potomac River.

This was one of the many stories told about Washington's strength and skill.

Here is a riddle from Civil War days:

Abraham Lincoln asked, "How many legs has a mule, if you call a tail a leg?"

The answer is four.

"Even if you call a tail a leg, it's still a tail," said Lincoln. He used this riddle to explain that just saying a thing is so does not make it so.

In the days of the old West
—who could boast that he was the greatest Indian fighter?
—who never used a saddle but rode faster and farther than the rest?
—who shot people, blew them up, then let them go home and hang themselves?

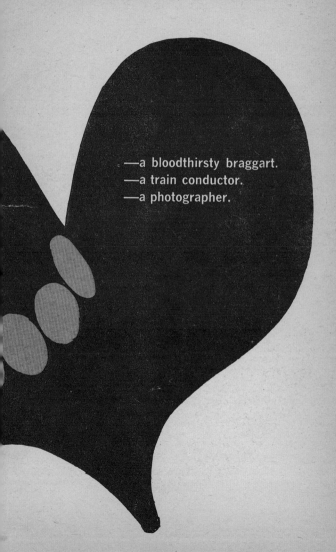

—a bloodthirsty braggart.
—a train conductor.
—a photographer.

Jeannette Rankin of Montana was elected to the House of Representatives in 1916 before Congress gave women the right to vote. How was that possible?

There was no law that kept women from running for office.

Montana women helped elect Jeannette Rankin. Their state had a law giving them the right to vote years before Congress granted this right to all American women.

What kind of bridges did the Russians use in World War II that were made without wood, stone or steel?

Bridges of ice.

One of these bridges helped save the city of Leningrad. In 1941 Leningrad was almost completely surrounded by German armies. But it did not surrender. When nearby Lake Ladoga froze, tracks were laid over the ice and trains ran on them, carrying supplies to the city.

Why do we seldom hear of the **Mayflower's** second trip to the New World?

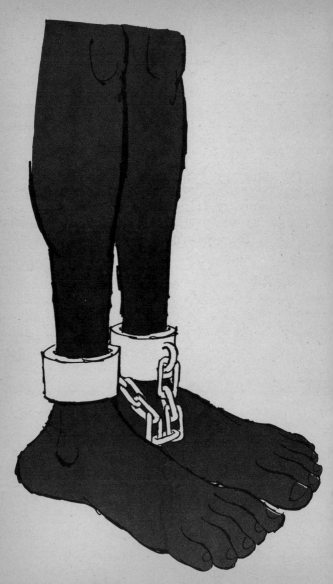

Because the Mayflower probably was used as a slave ship.

A boat by that name carried captive Africans to the West Indies, where they were sold as slaves.

Two Americans met in broad daylight. Before hundreds of witnesses one shot and killed the other. Yet the killer was never arrested and brought to trial. Why not?

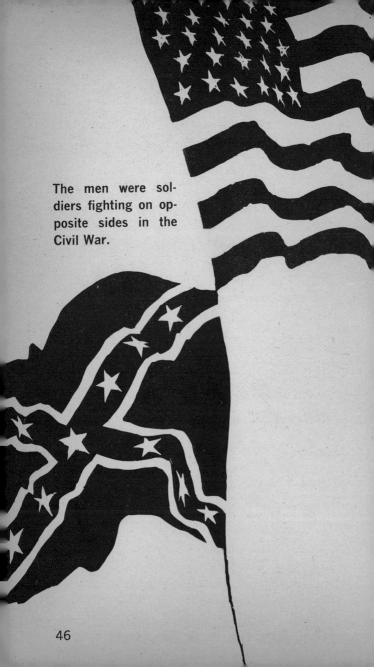

The men were soldiers fighting on opposite sides in the Civil War.

1. What ancient city was destroyed but never attacked?
2. What college began almost 200 years ago but has never had a graduating class?
3. What railroad had thousands of passengers but never any trains?
4. What ancient building was covered on top but never had a roof?
5. What author became world-famous but never wrote a single line?
6. What part of the world has been explored but never seen?

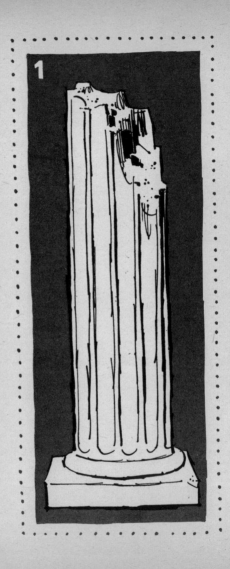

Pompeii.

This Roman city was destroyed by a volcano. It was buried under mud and ash when Mt. Vesuvius erupted in A.D. 79.

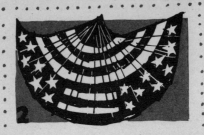

The Electoral College.

The president and vice president of the U.S. are not elected by direct vote of the people. They are chosen by the Electoral College, which is made up of 538 electors of the winning party in each state.

The Underground Railroad.

This was an escape system used by slaves who were making their way north to freedom. They traveled at night. Friends hid them by day at "stations" along the "railroad."

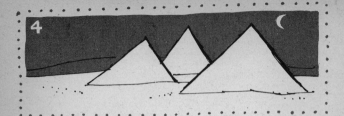

An Egyptian pyramid.

Homer.
Homer was a storyteller who lived in Greece before there was a written Greek language. His tales were passed from one generation to the next. Eventually they were collected and put in two great books, the *Iliad* and the *Odyssey*.

The deepest part of the ocean.

In places the ocean is about six miles deep. No one has ever gone down that far, but scientists have used sounding instruments to measure the depths and map the ocean bottom.

GEOGRAPHY

Where can you find
—roads without
  cars,
—forests without
  trees,
—cities without
  houses?

On a map.

According to the 1970 census, New York has the largest population of any city in the United States. What city is next to New York?

Yonkers.

It is on the northern border of New York City.

Denver

TALLAH

Springfield

LANSI

TRENTON

Austin

COLUM

Sacrament

Raleigh

ATLA

How can you name the capital of every state in the United States in less than a minute?

What can Japanese men do
that American men cannot do?

They can vote in Japanese elections.

Where do both ends of a compass needle always point north?

Any direction is north from that spot, and any way a compass needle points is north. There is no other direction at the South Pole.

When is a high mountain not a high mountain?

When most of it is underwater.

Several chains of high mountains rise from the ocean bottom. Many of them do not reach the surface, but the peaks of some stick out of the water, forming islands.

The Hawaiian Islands and many of the islands of the West Indies are the tops of undersea mountains over 20,000 feet high.

what kind of a place GETS BIGGER AS IT Gets smaller?

A ghost town.

When a town's factories or mines close down, people move away. Houses and stores become empty, forming a ghost town. This happened to many places in the West. The population became smaller and smaller, and as more and more buildings were abandoned, the ghost town grew.

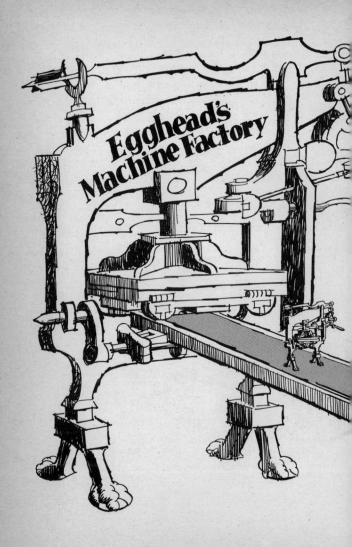

What factories make products
—that cut down pollution from cars?
—that go underwater without getting wet?
—that use nothing to do something?

Factories that make
—bicycles.
—engines for submarines.
—thermos jugs.

A thermos jug is really two jugs, one inside the other, with a space between them. The air has been pumped out of this space leaving "nothing"—a vacuum. Since a vacuum does not conduct heat, anything hot that is put in the jug stays hot, anything cold stays cold.

Sun	Mon	Tues
8	9	10

At the International Date Line.

That's where each calendar date begins officially. The Date Line runs through the Pacific Ocean at or near 180° Longitude. It lies in the first of· the earth's 24 time zones. Standard time is one hour earlier in the next zone to the west, and one hour earlier in each succeeding zone. Since there are 24 zones, the time in the last zone, just east of the line, is a whole day earlier. So if you travel eastward across the line you go back a day. Cross on Friday and it will be Thursday on the other side.

Potatoes.

The eyes on the outside are buds. They sprout underground and grow into potato plants.

Strawberries.

Their seeds are on the outside.

Honeybees.

They have six legs and are animals.

Goats.

Their kids are born with beards.

How can Indians tell what the weather will be without using weather instruments?

They listen to the forecasts.

PROFESSOR EGGHEAD'S GEOGRAPHY QUIZZLE

Where can you find:
1. A river that flows backward?
2. People who are neither black, white, red nor yellow?
3. Sand that is not sand?
4. Fresh water in the ocean?
5. People who travel but never leave home?
6. Seas that are not seas?

Where a river meets the sea.
The mouth of the river is really an arm of the sea. It has tides, just as the sea does. A rising tide sends water upstream and makes the river flow backward.

BRAZIL

In the upper Amazon region.
Settlers of all races came to this part of South America and intermarried. Now their grandchildren and great-grandchildren are not black, white, red or yellow but mixtures of all four races.

In sandstone.

Long ago sand settled on the bottom of the sea. As more and more piled up, the sand grains in the deeper layers were pressed and cemented together.

In time these layers became dry land. Where they show today, we find they are no longer sand but hard, solid sandstone.

In an iceberg.

The ice originally comes from the land, and is free of salt. It forms in mountains from piled-up layers of snow. Then it moves slowly down to sea as a glacier—a river of ice. Chunks break off from the glacier and float away as icebergs.

In a gypsy camp.
Gypsies travel in wagons or trucks which are their homes. Most of them never settle permanently in one place.

On the moon.
The dark patches on the
moon were once thought to
be bodies of water and were
called seas. We still call them
seas, though now we know
they are plains.

MATH

Once there was a lady who had five children, half of whom were boys. What were the other half?

Boys.

Ten feet times ten feet gives 100 square feet. But if you multiply ten shoes by ten shoes, what product do you get?

None.

You multiply numbers, not things. If you
want 100 square shoes, go to a shoe factory.

How can you draw
—a straight line that is curved?
—two straight lines without taking your pen-
  cil off the paper?
—two parallel lines that are not straight?

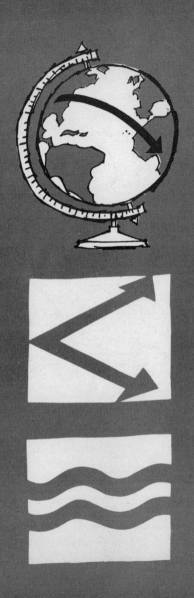

Use a globe.
Connect two points on the globe with the shortest possible line. You will draw a curve that will also be straight.

In math a straight line is one that takes the shortest path between two points.

Draw an angle.
The arms will be two straight lines each going in a different direction.

Draw two curved lines
with the same distance between them at every point. They will be parallel.

Suppose you have a million dollars and give away one quarter and another quarter and then another quarter. How much will you have left?

How can you
add holes to a pound
of Swiss cheese
without changing
its weight?

Slice the cheese.

1. What has no length, width or thickness, but can be measured?
2. Four to begin with, take away four, then eight are left. Eight what?
3. How can you draw a circle around a dog that the dog cannot get out of?
4. When is a cube not a cube?
5. How many times can seven be subtracted from 77?

Temperature.

Corners.
Cut off the four corners of a rectangle and you will have eight corners

e

Draw it on the dog.

THIS SIDE DOWN

102

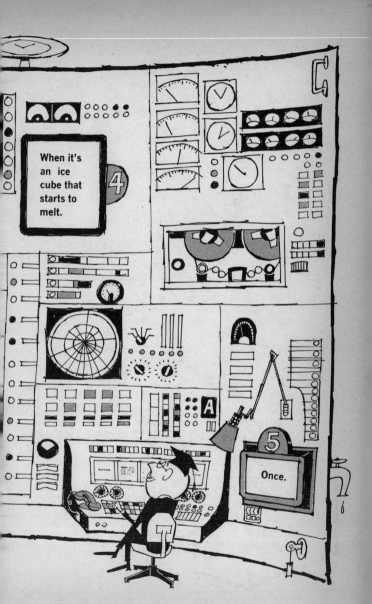

When it's an ice cube that starts to melt.

Once.

103

A board is to be cut in two pieces; but after cutting halfway through it on each side, there are still two feet to cut. How is that possible?

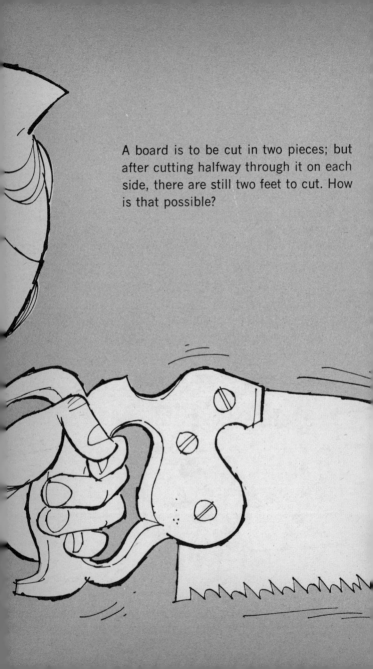

A plank four inches by four inches has nine holes an inch apart. How can the biggest square without holes be cut from the plank?

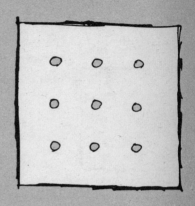

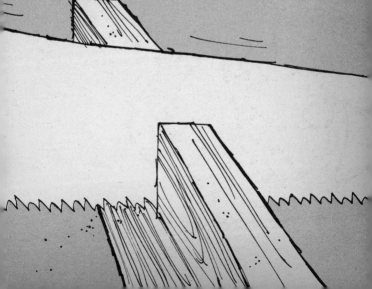

Like this:

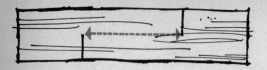

And like this:

A farmer who had 2½ piles of corn in one row and 1½ piles in another row decided to put them together. How many piles did he have?

One.

What kind of shape
—is made with four equal lines but is not a
  square?
—has four equal sides but is drawn with six
  lines?
—has an inside on the outside?
—has no beginning and no end but something in the middle?

—a diamond.
—a pyramid
made of four triangles.
—a doughnut shape,
which is called a torus. The inside hole is still on the outside.
—a sphere.

Why is a number
like a reptile?

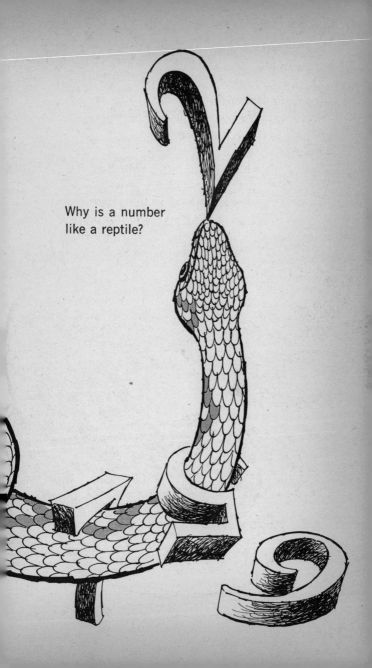

Because neither one is real.

Oh yes, a garter snake is a real animal that you can find and make a pet of. So is a wood turtle. Both belong to the reptile class. But you can't find and make a pet of the class. It does not exist as a real thing. It is just an idea.

And that's what a number is. Take three, for example. You can have three books, but take away the books and what happens to the three? It does not exist by itself. It is not a real thing—it is just an idea.

To count backwards from nine
just say one, two, three, etc.

a. How can you add three numbers to one and get two for the answer?
b. What number multiplied by eight gives eight?
c. When does seven come before one?
d. What number added to nine gives nine?
e. When do four fives equal six?
f. How can you count to ten in four steps if you count by threes?

a $1 + \frac{1}{3} + \frac{1}{3} + \frac{1}{3} = 2$

b

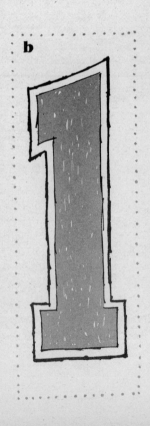

When you count the hours
from seven to one on a clock.

d
zero

e $\dfrac{55}{5} - 5 =$

f Start with the negative number −2. Add three for the next number and continue in this way until you get to 10.

$$-2+3+3+3+3=10$$

SCIENCE

Why is a dinosaur like an omelet?

**Because
it came from
an egg.**

Fossil eggs of about a dozen kinds of dinosaurs have been found so far.

Probably all dinosaurs came from eggs. Their nearest living relatives—alligators, crocodiles and lizards—all hatch from eggs.

What kind of mothers

—let their children gain 20 pounds a week?
—give their babies the least milk?
—hang their babies?
—keep their young on ice?

These animal mothers:

Elephants.
Their young grow fast. A 300-pound infant may weigh 1700 pounds at the age of three and 2800 pounds at four.

Shrews.
They are the smallest animals with milk. The mother weighs less than an ounce and has babies the size of bees.

Bats.
When a baby gets too heavy to carry, the mother hangs it up somewhere while she flies off to look for food.

Penguins.

The emperor penguin hatches in winter on Antarctic ice. The mother keeps her chick close to her, warming it with her body. Without this heat, the chick would die.

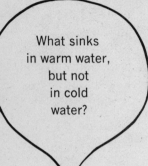

Cold water.

It sinks because it is heavier than warm water.

Try this:

Take a tall glass of warm water.

Fill a small bottle with colored cold water. Close the bottle with your thumb. Hold the bottle sideways and lower it into the glass. Then open the bottle.

Watch the colored cold water sink.

Take the gas in a tank, for example. It has no size or shape of its own. In the tank, it is compressed into a small space and it takes the shape of the tank.

But let the gas out. It expands in all directions, changing in size while it also changes in shape.

On its foot,
there is a head.
And on the head
are eyes.
The foot walks.
The head moves.
The eyes see.
A monster?
No—

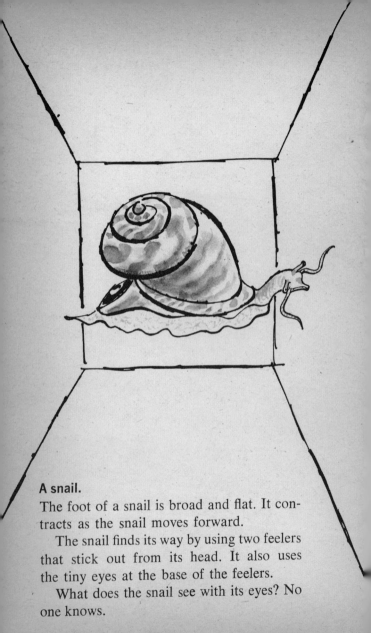

A snail.

The foot of a snail is broad and flat. It contracts as the snail moves forward.

The snail finds its way by using two feelers that stick out from its head. It also uses the tiny eyes at the base of the feelers.

What does the snail see with its eyes? No one knows.

What trees have more
water than wood in
their trunks?

What trees are really
grass?

What trees have
leaves on bare
branches?

Redwoods.

These trees have so much water in their trunks that fires do not kill them.

Redwoods grow in the rain forests of California and Oregon. Many live for centuries and become giants hundreds of feet tall.

Bamboo.

A bamboo stalk may grow as high as a two-story building. Yet it is a grass. Like the other plants in the grass family, its stem is jointed and the veins in its leaves all go in the same direction.

Trees that shed their leaves each fall.

Buds stay on the branches of these trees all winter. Tiny leaves are curled up inside the buds. They will come out in spring, when the buds open.

When can an astronaut's baby reach the sky?

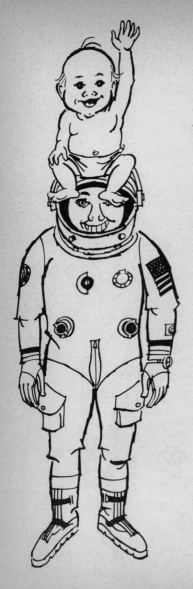

Any time,
for the sky
begins
at the ground.

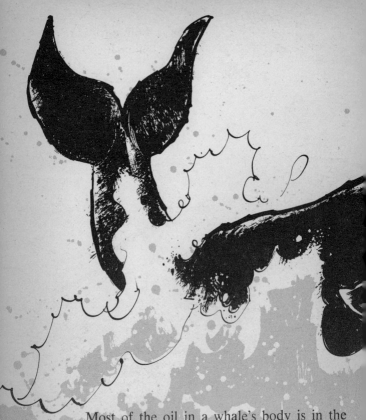

Most of the oil in a whale's body is in the blubber. This is a thick layer of fat under the skin. It keeps the whale warm.

The blubber of a blue whale, which is the largest whale, may yield 20 tons of oil. Long ago the oil was burned in lamps. Now soap and cosmetics are made from it in countries where whales are still hunted. In most countries, the hunting has been stopped to prevent whales from becoming extinct.

US INVENTIONS

A wheel.

A turning car wheel pushes back against the road. The road returns the push, making the wheel go forward.

You don't believe it? Run a toy automobile over a cardboard strip. The wheels go forward; the strip goes backward.

A gear.

Use a hand eggbeater and you turn a big gear that turns a little gear. The big gear moves slowly. While it makes one turn, the little gear makes five and goes five times as fast.

A gyroscope.

It has a heavy wheel that turns rapidly around an axis. This motion keeps the axis pointed in one direction. A gyroscope can keep a vehicle going straight forward. It is used in steering ships, planes and spacecraft.

A pulley.
Pull down one end of the rope and the other end goes up, lifting a weight.

Before Pluto was discovered, how many planets were there?

The same number as there are now.

At present we know of nine planets that go around the sun. Of these, Pluto is the farthest from us. It was discovered in 1930.

1. What has no voice but hums?
2. What has no legs but walks?
3. What has no mouth but eats?
4. What has no ears but hears?
5. What has no lungs but breathes?

1. A bumblebee.

"Bzz," it hums. The sound comes from its wings. They vibrate when the bee flies.

2. The starfish.

When walking, one of its rays takes the lead. The tip curls up, then pushes out. The ray contracts and the starfish slides slowly forward.

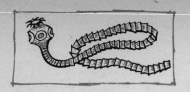

3. A tapeworm.

This animal does not need a mouth,
for it takes in food through its skin.
A tapeworm lives in the intestines of
other animals, soaking up food digested
by them. It is a parasite.

4. A daddy longlegs.

Its second pair of legs have sense
organs on them. They pick up sounds,
although the daddy longlegs walks on
them, too. If alarmed, it lifts one of
those legs and stops to listen.

5. A fish.

Fish breathe through gills. They take
in oxygen that is dissolved in water.

What is full when it is empty?

FULL & EMPTY

A pop bottle
after all the soda is gone.

The bottle looks empty, but it is full—full of air.

Turn the bottle upside down. Then lower it into a tank of water. Hold the bottle at a slant and air bubbles out.

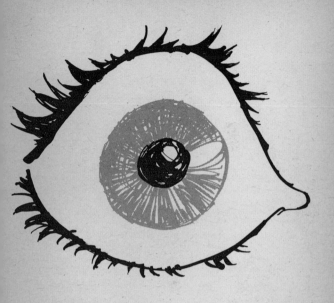

Who can't see something that is
in front of his nose
but
can look in his ear with his eye?

You.

You can't see the air in front of you. But you can see into your ear.

Stand with your left side toward a mirror. Hold another mirror in your right hand and tilt it. Hold it high enough and you can look into your left ear.

PROFESSOR EGGHEAD'S SCIENCE QUIZZLE

1. When is a nut not a nut?
2. When is a flying saucer not a flying saucer?
3. When is a flower not a flower?
4. When is a year not a year?
5. When is a color not a color?
6. When is a heavenly body not a heavenly body?

When it is a peanut.

A nut has just one seed in the shell. A peanut has two. The plant on which it grows belongs to the pea family. Its shell is really a pea pod and the "nuts" inside are really peas.

2. When it is identified.

The mysterious spots of light that people call flying saucers or Unidentified Flying Objects can usually be explained. Scientists find that most of them are due to searchlights on clouds, reflections from weather balloons or electrical discharges somewhat like ball lightning.

When a flying saucer cannot be explained, it is generally because the time and place of the sighting were not accurately reported.

When it is a daisy.
A daisy is really a little bouquet. The yellow center is made of hundreds of tiny flowers that bloom separately.

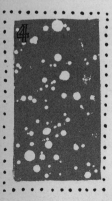

When it is a light-year.
Astronomers use the light-year as a unit measuring the distance between stars. It is the distance light travels in a year.

Light travels 186,000 miles in one second, so a light-year is very large. How large? About six trillion (6,000,000,000,000) miles.

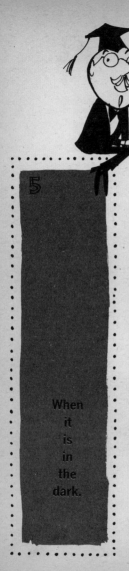

5

When
it
is
in
the
dark.

6

When you are on it.

When you are on the Earth, it does not seem to be in the sky. But if you were on the moon, you would see the earth shining in the sky above. You would see it as a heavenly body.